BEHIND CLOSED EYES

Micae'la Mone'

BEHIND CLOSED EYES

None of the dreams that I have behind closed eyes would be possible without God and my grandparents. My grandmother and grandfather have loved me unselfishly. They have gone beyond being grandparents to me. The words I possess aren't beautiful enough to paint them. Mere words could never thank them. I dedicate this book to you MawMaw and Papa.
I love you!

Acknowledgments

I would like to thank everyone who has supported me through this process. You're encouraging words, prayers, and support has meant the world to me. I would especially like to thank Roger Raymond for believing in my dream. I am forever grateful for your time and help. My life has been a journey and without God I would be lost. All glory and honor to him.

Table of Contents

CLOSED EYES

Fried Chicken Blues

While mopping floors one night, dipping the mop like it was my heart in and out of dirty water, I held my tears back. I placed a smile on my face that entire night as strangers ordered chicken and rice dressing. I read their stories as their indecisive eyes studied an invariable menu. I watched as their lips would part to order the same thing as they did before. Dr. Pepper, Coke, Strawberry. Medium, Large. 162, 162, ma'am your order is ready. Thank you, Goodnight! Those were my lines. I held tears back as I mopped that place with my heart.

Defeated Black Man

There he stands head down crumbling inside

Trying to grip the years that steady roll by

He inhales, exhales tempted to die

Because it's been hell living his life

But, yet he fights

This cold war has turned a man full of ambitions

Into old leftovers in Uncle Sam's kitchen

You can find old pictures of him in photo albums standing tall

in combat boots

Inhaling life in a military suit

Too bad life isn't like Kodak

His mind is trapped in Iraq

I wait for him to come back

I'll always love you poor dad.

Crying for Shaniya

Last night I cried. As I took my shower tears fell from my eyes
and I cried
I stood naked crying in my shower and all I could do was think
about her
I saw her eyes and her smile
Sweet and serene
I saw hope for tomorrow; I saw things that she would never be
able to see
And I cried
I cried because I saw her face on my TV screen with words in
yellow "CHILD FOUND DEAD"
I cried because she died before she could know there were such
things as danger lying ahead
And I cried, God I cried
Because I wanted to save her but it was too late
I wanted to hug her and make things better but, it was too late
She should be playing Barbie right now but, she is dead
She should be dancing like clouds are underneath her but, she is
dead

She should be eating candy and watching cartoons past eight but,

she is dead

Where she should be playing it is silent

Where she should be lying it is still

Where she should be dreaming it is waiting for her sleepy head

Where she was loved it is hurting

Where she should be it is forever broken

I'm praying to God there are toys in heaven for her to play

Praying to God there's always a smile on her face

I cried last night because a child was found dead

CHILD SOLD INTO PROSTITUTION BY MOTHER is what

my screen read

Crying tears for Shaniya shouldn't have to be said

Sleep baby girl sleep

Humidity

A beat similar to distant drums lifts from my feet only to
surround the air around me.

A steady beat as I run through a summer's night heat
Thick Louisiana air
Moist from its children's despair
And it soaks me as I run through someone's heartbreak
It chokes me as I run through a slaves wail
There's nothing like thick Louisiana air
The steady beat that flows from my feet keeps me going
The further I run the more my soul is pouring
Releasing emotions into a summer's dark night
Without saying a word I share my entire life
Inevitably I've become one with this thick Louisiana air.

MOMENT OF SILENCE

As she stared at the paper in her hand
She felt her soul crumble inside
Breaking piece by piece she felt it as it died.
And the words wouldn't come from her mouth
She was grasping for them
Gasping for them
Yet she stood silent.--

And like a silent storm she began to hear his whispers in her ear.
"I love you and I'll always be here"

But she was alone
And his deadly whispers were all she could hear.
At once she fell as if the world was dropping on her.
She hit the ground meeting her despair
Then the words came slicing through the air
WHY!!?
You would swear levees broke the way her tears flowed.
WHY, again piercing all of her inside.

She couldn't fathom the idea that she now carried death inside.

It wasn't until now that she realized

She had been gambling with her life.

A beautiful freshman in college

Former beauty queen

All-around American girl now diagnosed with HIV

This is more than a disease this is a harsh reality

It's stealing away dreams and replacing them with tragedies

Early obituaries and premature cemeteries

 Leaving mothers up late nights crying Hail Mary's

Yes as she looked at the paper

It felt as if her whole world was coming to an end

Couldn't believe this was happening.

    So take heed to the story that I'm telling

    So next time it won't be you on the floor yelling

    It's time we come together and say:

    R.I.P. to HIV

-- This is your moment of silence

LABOR PAINS

Doesn't everybody like a beautiful piece of art?
One drawn with the colors of the heart
Instead of a paintbrush I have an ink pen
Listen closely as my painting begins

Woman...
Pacing back and forth talking to her friends
Stomach swollen from the life growing within
Sharp pain... makes her stop in her tracks
Tightness as she begins to contract

Now they're rushing, running, grabbing bags
Time is moving forward, never turning back
As they loaded up the vehicle and started on their way
She tilted her head, closed her eyes and visited a yester place
  A yester-place where yesterdays
   Were filled with hard work and never any play
Where it seemed that her dreams were so very far away
But yet so close she could always taste
The sweetness of them kind of like her grandmother's pies
A slice of paradise tucked between two white clouds

19

That's what she kept in the back of her head
Every night as she prayed on the side of her bed

"Dear Lord......"
He heard every word that she prayed
He kept building her wings
Stronger until she could fly away

The door opens
"Ma'am are you okay?"
Her eyes open
"Yes.... I've been waiting for this day".

Forever... Never really is that far away
It was even closer as they wheeled her down the hospital's
hallway
Once in the room they got her I.V.'s going
Checked her vitals, got the Demerol rolling

Contractions growing Closer and Closer
Her friends see her in pain; don't know how to console her
She's turning to her left and then back to her right
Clinging to the rail holding on for dear life
The doctor checks her; she's only five-centimeters
Five more to go before he has a front-seater

Before he exits the door she begins to overflow
Her waters come rushing like waves against African shores
The time is now the wait is no more

Anticipation consumes the room
The silence is as loud as in King Tut's tomb
For in the Queen's womb
The most sacred fruit
Has ripened to the point that it must bloom

Her thighs are shaking; nails digging deeper
Cries filling the ceiling to her soul's keeper
The doctor says push and she pushes with all her might
This is the moment she has been waiting for all of her life

And it looks like heaven has opened its skies
As that slice of paradise slowly begins to arrive

Deep breath and she pushes again
Push… With everything she's holding within

With every tear that she's cried
Everything that she's believed
Every battle that she's fought…
All of her heartbeats

It's a perfect delivery
And you've just witnessed the birth of a dream.

Everything Will Be Alright

Everything will be alright that's what he said
As she laid crying in the bed
While the growing fetus in her stomach had no idea of what lied
ahead

"Sometimes you gotta do what you gotta do"
That's what he told her
As she listened over the phone he never tried to console her

"I'm down on my knees begging"
That's what he cried out
But he never heard the words that came out of her mouth
And like a fool she listened to him
Just like before when the lights were dim
This time he wasn't there
He didn't hear her despair

Today she realized he'll never be there

He'll forget what happened on the twelfth with the passing years
But she'll always remember what he planted in her ear
Everything will be all right—

Lost In Words

I'm confined in my thoughts that scream so loudly in my head
In black and white memories set to a background that is red

And I try to escape.

I constantly feel like a small dot of ink that falls from my pen
Oblivious to the rest of the world
Plagued by what everyone's thinking
And I'm captured in what's inside of me
Gradually trying to say what I constantly see

And I try to escape

It feels as if every part of me is filled with words
Words trying to escape begging to be heard
My soul is lost within the rhythm
It's terrible that I'm the only one that hears them
I'm lost in words and I can't find my way out
Lost and no one knows I'm missing
How will I get out?

Lost and yet I really don't want to be found.

Inside Out

I can't sing a note, but I can write a song

I haven't been to Hollywood, but the stage is my home

Those that know me and know me well

Know that just to get to heaven with bruised knees I'll crawl

through hell

In the face of opposition I keep my pumps on

No, I can't sing a note, but this is my song

Written with a pen dipped in tears

And a heart broken by unforgiving years

I've flipped myself inside out to show you how I feel.

Forever writing until the day he calls me home.

I can only pray my words will live on.

Until then I remain inside out.

I WILL FATHER YOU

I'm like a vessel lost at sea in the midst of a storm. I've been battered by the winds and blown off course. Despite my turmoil I sustain. I sustain because clouds do part and the sun will shine. I sustain because who knows where the wind will blow me. I sustain because he hasn't left me.

Prayer for You

I said a prayer for you last night
A prayer that by daylight
All of your trouble would be out of sight
    And that the Lord would make it right

I said a prayer for you last night and I know he heard my call
Because His word says that He will carry us if ever we should fall
Yes, I said a prayer for you last night
    And I prayed with my all

I said a prayer for you last night
And tonight I'll do the same
The Lord will heal us all
We just have to call on his name
For He is The One who forgives sinners
And the One who heals the lame

    Yes, I said a prayer for you last night.

PREDESTINED

I believe everybody can be GREAT and everybody has a DESTINY! Whether you arrive to that destination depends solely on you. We are all predestined to succeed and leave our own mark. The path that we chose to journey determines our outcome. If we constantly search outside of ourselves for happiness, love, and completion we will never find it. Our body is our temple and God exists within us. The true answers and directions to your destiny lie within you. No, not everyone will be millionaires or celebrities but everybody can live a fruitful life if they allow themselves to. No obstacle is too great to overcome. A lot of our situations are products of our own decisions and not his. We stumble when we feel that we know what's best and not him. God will guide you to the right path but it is your decision to travel it. In life yes there are storms but they are only growing periods. Sometimes when you grow there are growing pains.... trust and stand fast. You are GREAT and PREDESTINED! If the road you've been traveling leads to many dead ends and flat tires perhaps it's because you're lost. Seek God he knows the way! God bless and be fruitful! Grow!

Thoughts on Yesterday

Excuse me isn't it true that yesterday's gone?
If that is so, then why do you mourn?

Why do you feed on yesterdays left-over;
when today's meal is growing colder?
Weep and cry, scream and howl
Yesterday's gone
So please move on

If you live on yesterday,
Then your past is your future
It's like a broke car going nowhere in neutral

Today is the present so open it as a gift
Every day is a new day
So choose smartly how you live
The past can consume
Be careful of what you do

Look back and reflect, laugh and learn
Don't let it define you because you may get burned

BEHIND CLOSED EYES

Today is here,

Yesterday's behind

Tomorrow is in front of you

Think with your spirit and not your mind

Excuse me, today's almost gone

Tomorrow's not promised so where are you going?

Dear Haiti

Faces like mine flashing on the TV screen
Crying to God wondering what all of this means
Buildings crumpled, bodies lifeless
The only color I see is red flowing from this crisis
I sit watching in awe as I pray to God.

Dear brother, Dear sister
I will get on my knees and pray with you
I can hear your crying; I can see your dying
Please hold on tight to your faith and keep fighting

Oh Haiti! Dear Haiti!
We've been thinking about you lately

The ground may shake, the ground may break
But our Father above hears every word that you pray

Dear Haiti, Dear Haiti
I will never forget your faces.

God Bless

God's Child

You tried to defeat me. In your quest you waged a war for my soul strapping yourself with heavy artillery. Yes, you tried to break me; you and your lies. It was you who said I was ugly, talentless, and weak. It was you who said no one could love me. It was you who said the world was against me. It was you and only you who wanted me dead. Your lies didn't work. I am beautiful, talented, and strong. I am loved and living. You did not defeat me because I gave my battle to my Lord. It is he who won my victory and saved me! He is my father and you are a lie! Forever I am God's child.

Katrina

Sometimes I feel like Katrina is inside of me
100 mph winds trying to devour me

But still I stand

Despite the struggle, the pain, and the sorrow
Despite the sadness, the rain, I'm still fighting to see tomorrow

When the waters start to rise and my levees dare to break
When my soul feels like fleeing I hold on to my faith
Because I'll only have to endure for a storm
Before he lifts me by my arm and holds me like I've just been born

Sometimes I feel like Katrina is inside of me
But I'm still standing because God walks beside me.

Self Examination

Would you know love if she looked you dead in your eyes?

Would you know Jesus if he happened to pass by?

Children starving in Africa dangling onto their lives

While the rest of us play blind living our lives

One day we all say we will change

But the days keep passing and we remain the same

So the next time you look into the mirror look a little deeper

Look into your soul and realize you are your brother's keeper

So if tomorrow doesn't come and you're inhaling your last breath

You can look him in the eyes and say Lord I didn't live for myself

Because that's the only way we will live eternally

By going through this life living unselfishly

Dear God

Dear God,

Today wasn't my day. I've been broken in every way. I tried to smile, but my tears fell down. I know heaven heard them as they hit the ground. I want to fight but giving in is easy. I hear your words that you will never leave me. I know the devil is my only enemy... So dear Lord I beg please win my victory!

LETTERS TO MY SONS

To My Unborn Son:

Every day now, I can feel you growing inside of me. I can feel you moving and anticipating the outside world. Even though I haven't seen your face I LOVE YOU! I know that you're mine. Every morning and night I pray that you're healthy. I pray that I won't fail you. Once you do arrive it's important that I raise you right. I want you to have every chance that I didn't have. The most important thing that I want you to learn is to live your life for the Lord and to never let what people say or do compromise you. I want you to be a strong black man and to respect women. I also want you to have a mind of your own and not to let others poison you. No matter what I will always love you and be by your side.

Love,

MOMMY

LIFELINE

One day you'll travel through time by the way of your thoughts
and remember our moments together.

A smile will tip toe onto your faces as you will recall our games of
nose, eyes, ears, and mouth.

You'll remember countless hours of Thomas the Train
And fighting amongst each other for tracks
As time passes there will come a time when I will no longer be
able to magically treat your bobo's
And my kisses will no longer stop tears
As time passes life will begin its journey with you
I have no idea of what the future may hold.

I am not a fortune teller, but there are a few things that I do
know.

Heartbreak is inevitable, but its pain isn't forever.

In life sometimes we play both roles so always be mindful.

This world is a forever changing stage with a constant back drop.

I pray that yours is always set to God.

I know that, as you will transition from boys to men, there will
come a time when I must let you fly.

I also understand that as a woman I can't teach you completely
about being a man.

However, I can teach you how to love and to be loved. I can
teach you how to respect and to be respected. I can teach you

when to lead and when to follow. I can teach you things such as responsibility, trust, and loyalty. I may not be a man, but I can raise you to be a great one!

One day you'll look back and realize that our lifeline was never cut at birth....

No our lifeline survives for a lifetime.

I love you boys.

Franko's Eyes

In the middle of my demise while waiting for Jesus to rise

I found peace in my son's eyes

A peace that took over me

A peace that was mine to keep

No matter what is brought my way

I will be okay

I could have been in Baghdad when Clinton dropped bombs

But would have suffered no harm

Or stood in the middle of New Orleans when the waters rose

And still emerged with dry clothes

No matter what is brought my way

Yes, I will be okay

Because I've found peace in Franko's eyes

While waiting for Jesus to rise

Dallas Mornings

On the weekends, when the sun rises on our lateness, your kisses awaken me.

Your smiling face is as bright as the sun, peeping through my curtains, warming my soul.

You are my blessing.

Exactly, what I need to grow.

Your lips speak the sweetest words I know…

Mama, Mama, Mama

I love you Dallas.

One day our mornings will be a thing from the past.

I just hope that you keep them in your heart where they can last.

No matter how tall you get, no matter your age

You will always be my baby for the rest of my days.

You are my Dallas mornings without leaving the state.

Breathing

I could have lied down and let life have its way with me. I could have stayed lost when I began to go astray. With all of the strikes against me he still made a way. Every reason I had to give in is every reason why I'm still here fighting. I have two sons that I have to show how to be kings. This isn't about making it; it's about living. I'm breathing, I'm breathing, I AM BREATHING!

DRINKING FROM LOVE

God's Song

Love is a melody that only God can compose

Love is a melody its notes are within our soul

He dips his pen in sunsets so that his notes are always warm

Yes, love is a melody for it is God's song.

Today I heard a melody

So beautiful and sweet

I heard a song playing as two became one beat

My sister is singing I can see it in her smile

She's always had wings but today she truly flies

Love is a melody that only God can compose

It's a piece of heaven singing now within their souls.

Prototype

I think he's the prototype…. Just right
That sunset before a dark night…. That light
And he doesn't even know it yet
He's the type of Jon Doe that you can't forget
And he's free… I can tell by his wings
His soul speaks without saying a thing

That's the beauty in him
Shining when all else is dim
He's free, but I can't interfere with the wind.

He must be the prototype; that sunset before a dark night.

Flashback

Sitting outside late one night
I started thinking about my life
About how things are and how they have been
I started to remember the who, what, where, how, and when
That's when I thought of you as if you were here now
That's when the tears started to roll down
I miss you in so many ways that I can't begin to say
You've gone on but, never really went away

Flashback

And just like that you're back

Flashback

And just like that we're back

Back together again
Tell me where time went my friend

Flashback

Louisiana Temperatures

There's something about you that excites me

That gets my heart pumping blood

Rushing and Adrenaline rising

High like the temperatures on a hot July Louisiana day

Hey, could you bring some shade my way

There's no rushing into things because there's no race to be run

We're just here in the mix of things

enjoying the feeling of a love just begun.

And it feels Oh so good

You bathing my body with your touch

I wish I could frame each one of these moments up

And hang them proudly on my wall

Because your love is a work of art

It makes my temperatures rise like a hot Louisiana day even if it's

the middle of winter.

Waves

I'm riding these waves of yours until I wash up on distant shores

Where I hope the coast is nice

And you're always by my side

I'm riding these waves of yours

Who could ever want more?

Sisters

When I was younger I would always pray for a sister. I was the only child for seven years and when I finally did get a sibling it was a brother. My mom told me she wasn't having anymore children after him. It's funny how God works because two years and many miles later I met her. My parents divorce allowed us to cross paths.

God gave me a sister when I needed her the most. I was the new kid in class and she rode the same bus as me. I can still remember her asking me one day, "Why are you always looking down when you get on the bus?" As time passed she understood why without me having to tell her. She understood that I was hurt inside and struggled to pretend that everything was alright. Throughout the years we rode the same country, dusty bus together. Every year like clockwork I would get the same assigned seat like the year before. We shared great times on that long bus ride to and from school. Yes, God gave me a sister when I needed her the most. He knew that we would need each other.

Not only did God bless me with one sister he blessed me with two. A year after I met my first sister I met my second one. Back then we had no idea that we would be so close. God has a reason for everything. The three of us were the "country girls". We had sleepovers, played basketball together, shared secrets, laughs, and dreams. Our bond was unbreakable.

Looking back I smile when I think of our secret trips to Lake Charles when we should have been at school. I still have all of our pictures from school dances, Greenjackets, and everything else in between. Our memories together are endless. We know each other's first love and first heartbreak. We were there for one another during highs and lows. I thank God for giving me sisters like them.

We have transitioned from girls to women. In our labors we comforted one another. As we journey we support one another. Recently one of my sisters got married. I cried tears of joy as she was walked down the aisle. I cried those tears because she was complete. Even though we have grown up to live our own lives we will forever be sisters.

Now when we go out, to shoot pool or just to hang out with one another, we take the country route back home. We take the longer route so that we may laugh a little bit longer with each other. I thank God for the two of them because he knew I couldn't make this journey alone. I love you Brandi and Denise. I hope I can be the same sister that you have been to me.

Georgia Boy Blues

I saw a picture of you before I ever met you. I can
remember waking up in the middle of the night to see the
brother that I had patiently waited for. For months I wrote
about you in my journal in school. My daily journal entry in third
grade was dedicated to you and my occasional alien stories.
There wasn't a more proud sister than me. So, if you didn't know
it I loved you before you were here. I loved you when you were
that "something" in mom's belly that I couldn't yet understand.
As a matter of a fact they tried to explain it to me while I was
watching Touch By an Angel. In a way you were my angel and I
was going to be yours.

When you were a baby I use to sing to you. I would sing every
Disney song that I knew. I would recite every Annie and Wizard
of Oz line. Those were the things I would do with you before we
had to part ways. Sometimes I feel guilty because I believe I
cheated you out of a big sister. While I was drowning in my own
tears I forgot about you. I assumed that you would always be
okay. Looking back I wish I would have stayed so that you could
have run to me when someone may have picked on you at
school. I wish I could have been there to know more of your
secrets and listen to your stories instead of always writing mine.

Now you're a Georgia boy going through adolescence. I wish I
was there to help you or even knew how to. You're at that point
where you feel like the world is on your shoulders. No longer a
boy and yet still not a man. I know you look into the mirror and
can't help but to see a man that you never really knew. I wish I
had all of the answers but, life doesn't always give them. I wish I
could make you understand that it's not always hard and these are
merely growing pains. Just a stage you must go through in order
to become a man. I worry that the lines your IPod plays will
confuse you. Words are dangerous sometimes especially, the

words hidden in the melody of a rap line. Many of those lines teach you lies. There's a fine line between poison and art. Good thing our mama didn't raise any fools.

Right now I think it's safe to say you have those Georgia Boy Blues. It's nothing that you can't get through. Just like you I once had the weight of the world on my shoulders too. Just like you I had many questions with no answers. The same mirrors you are peering into now I peered into them too. The good news is that time does change your view. Even though we are miles and miles apart I am still your big sister. If ever you need me you can run to my heart. Life is still young waiting to be lived. It's only the Georgia boy blues messing with you kid.

I love you Rho.

Miss Angie

Miss Angie
I'm sorry for all of the tears that I made you cry before
This time when you cry it's going to be for joy
And Miss Angie
I made it through the storm
Lord knows you know how it use to pour
Miss Angie
I'm going to thank you like I never did before
I love you mom…

When I was younger I use to put on your shoes and pretend I
was just like you
I would put all of your rings on my fingers even though they were
loose
Please, don't be mad because I may have even lost a few
Just one or two
 That was years ago and now I must wear my own shoes
In my stride sometimes I think back to me and you

I can remember early mornings begging you not to brush my
sides
And crying not to go to the sitter; I never wanted to leave your
side
And I can remember hopping from bed to bed late at nights
And sleeping on your chest until I was almost five
These are the memories that I will carry for the rest of my life.

Miss Angie
I'm sorry for all of the tears that I made you cry before
This time when you cry it's going to be for joy
And Miss Angie
I made it through the storm
Lord knows you know how it use to pour
Miss Angie
I'm going to thank you like I never did before
I love you mom…

Do you remember in Germany how we would watch recorded
tapes?
The Cosby's, Michael Jackson, and Fat Albert would light up my
face
I think we even had a boot leg of The Little Mermaid
Grandma use to ship us a box of Rescue 911
I would sit hypnotized not making a sound

It seems like yesterday when I was singing every M.J. song and
dreaming of being on Barney
Do you remember the P.C.J. contest and how my hair was so
pretty?
That year the entire neighborhood showed up for my fifth
birthday party.
That same year right across the street a girl got hit
I still remember how you ran out to help… there's no
questioning where I got it.

Miss Angie

I'm sorry for all of the tears that I made you cry before
This time when you cry it's going to be for joy

And Miss Angie

I made it through the storm
Lord knows you know how it use to pour
Miss Angie
I'm going to thank you like I never did before
I love you mom…

The summer before first grade I had a Barbie bike. I always
wanted to ride as fast as the boys.
I still remember when I flipped it screaming in pain without a
voice
Just like now you picked me up like a giant and held me.
Mom, it seems like yesterday when we would eat at red lobster.
Every single time I would order spaghetti

I use to only want to eat devil squares, Doritos, Chinese, hot
wings and pickles…. Even though it would make me sick
Sometimes, (every now and then) you would let me
Every summer you would spend 5 hours braiding my hair. I'd
fall asleep with my head on your leg
When you were finished you would carry me to my bed

Miss Angie

I'm sorry for all of the tears that I made you cry before
This time when you cry it's going to be for joy
And Miss Angie
I made it through the storm
Lord knows you know how it use to pour
Miss Angie
I'm going to thank you like I never did before
I love you mom...

Phenomenal Woman was the first poem that I learned because you taught it to me.

It was you who introduced me to words and encouraged me to speak.

My pen has you to thank for uniting it with sheets.

It's true we've had our ups and downs
It was our downs that has made us even closer now

Often times I wish I could go back to nights of you reading to
me Addy.

I'm still that girl in pigtails pretending I'm Whitney.

I know that time can never be replaced

I find peace in knowing that the memories we have can never be
erased.

So, this time when you cry there will be tears of joy on your face.

Miss Angie

Miss Angie

I love you Mom.

RECYCLED TEARS

*If I could wash today away
I'd stand in the shower until it
dripped away. I pray to God to
wipe these tears away. If I could
wash today away.*

Recycling Bin

Maybe if you would have been the first I would have cried longer

But, sorry sweetie I cried those tears for someone else

Maybe if my heart was whole to begin with you could have had

the satisfaction in breaking it

But, sorry sweetie he did that before you too

So, the tears that I did cry weren't even for you

They were recycled tears from a past lived through you.

Excuse me while I empty my bin.

Raising Kings

Broken is the heart of the son whose father says no, you can't come with me today.

Heavy is the soul of the mother as he turns and walks away.

Her eyes filled with tears that her heart beats;

Suffocating inside from the words that her son speaks

My daddy said no.

She is a Queen raising Kings in a land of no sympathy

But she teaches them love

She is a Queen raising Kings in a land of hostility

But she teaches them peace

She is a Queen raising Kings in a land of broken dreams

But she teaches them to believe

I am a Queen raising Kings

My Father is our victory.

She

She was in love with he
He loved her, but her wasn't She
So they could never be
Fairy-tale happily
But how could this be?
When he was her king
Just remember in life
Nothing's ever what it seems
And he killed her dream
Took hold of her esteem
Now Her heart is numb
Her heart is cold
She'll never love again
Because her heart was stole
Yes She was in love with he
But he loved her –
and her wasn't she.
All that is left is this broken story.

Condemnation Emancipation

My flesh has hate for you

But my God says pray for you

I hold my tongue but sometimes my words escape through

Because pain never grows old it always feels brand new

Bruises may fade, scrapes may heal

Scars are forever its reminder on the heart is real

Every time I look at you with anger I do fill

On bending knees I'm praying to God please show me how to deal

If it's my eyes please cleanse them dear Lord

So that I may see the way that you see him Lord.

If it's my heart open it dear Lord to release what's within that's causing me to sin Oh Lord.

If it's my tongue please pass me your cup

So that I may drink from it and taste on your love

Because the hate that I have for him

Is killing me deep Lord, from within

Sorry but I have to release you…. I can no longer hate you

No, instead I will pray for you

Dear Lord, forgive them for they know not what they do.

YESTERDAY

I'm leaving yesterday behind me
I don't know why I was in love with it

Yesterday would always make me cry
But somehow I needed it

It was like the more that happened on yesterday
The longer I would stay in it

The more drama that went down
The longer I would play in it

After all of these years
I've finally caught up with today
Even in today I'm wiping yesterday's tears away

I'm leaving yesterday behind me
I wonder if it'll leave me

Today I'm writing about yesterday
And tomorrow I'll write about today

In the meantime I'm wiping yesterday's tears away

DELUSIONAL

FOR THE LAST 13 YEARS I'VE BEEN PLAYING HIDE
AND SEEK
MORE LIKE SEEKING AND NEVER FINDING THE
WAY THAT YOU'VE HIDDEN FROM ME
FALSE LOVE IS WHAT YOU GAVE ME
AND NOW I'M DESPERATE TO FIND MY INNER PEACE
I FEEL LIKE MY LIFE IS ON PAUSE AT TEN
STILL A CHILD HURT, ALONE, AND CRYING
IN THE MIDST OF MY TEARS I'M RUNNING TRYING
TO FIND WHERE YOU'RE HIDING
I'VE BEEN DONE COUNTING SO TELL ME WHERE
HAVE YOU BEEN

SEEKING YOU IN EVERY LOVE BUT IT'S NOT YOU
SO CONVINCED THAT I'VE CAUGHT YOU
WILL THIS PAIN EVER UNDO
DEAR FATHER WHERE ARE YOU

ALL OF THIS SEEKING AND NEVER FINDING HAS
TURNED ME COLD

CONSTANTLY SEARCHING THROUGH MY PAST IS
GETTING REAL OLD
BUT IT'S GOT A REAL GRASP; A TIGHT ASS HOLD
LOOK AT WHAT I'VE BECOME... IT'S A STORY TO BE
TOLD

Breathe

My pen twirls back and forth
As it twirls I see memories of before
They stand silently at my door
I don't know if it's the fact that they don't speak
Or the fact that they're here that has left me weak

My fan is circling off air of a yesterday
I can smell it; a scent of bittersweet
It's everywhere
Yesterday, that is but, why has it come to visit me

Is it because I shut my door never to open it again?
Or because I shun the thought of being its friend?
 How can I ignore yesterday when it has run into today?
It's chasing me relentlessly; I can't get away

So am I suppose to shake hands and call it truce
Or sit here watching it mock me as its fool?

I choose to do neither instead I breathe
Because yesterday will never own me. They're only memories; not
my reality.

Russian Through Love

He's playing a game of rushing through love; a game of Russian
roulette
He's had a lot of close calls but, hasn't lost yet
All bets are up; all eyes on him
He has too much pride; his only concern is to win
Here he goes again
Her heart's open wide

CLICK

I guess it's safe to open our eyes
Because his damsel is still alive
Barely holding on to life
As she silently dies inside

Now she feels as if her life has no meaning
 Because he took her heart from her still beating
And he's still needing
Because he's lost all touch of feeling

Rushing through love each pull a lost
Rushing through love wishing the roulette would collect its cost
He's rushing through love

CLICK
CLICK
BOOM

SOUTHERN COMFORT

ODE TO THE DREAM

A bush shakes as he runs by

Every move calculated; every step precise

      He inhales the thick air of his land

And exhales it again

Stories are etched in his face

Battles in his hands

A Strong African Warrior... on the pride lands

is where he stands

That is until the ships came and the chains locked

The pride stripped and the rains dropped

      The heavens cried when he was taken away

      The heavens cried as aloud he prayed

He was packed away, confined and restricted...

Traveling the sea to foreign lands

      Where he would no longer be allowed

      to be a Strong African Man

As the waves rocked back and forth he dreamed of Africa

      Her drums calling his name

He dreamed of Africa

He dreamed of his throne

Once the ships docked and light poured in
He realized much of his people were no longer breathing
   He was no longer free
   Instantly sold into slavery
He worked fields until his hands would bleed
Never daring to pause and get down on one knee
   Because the whip was always near
   Breaking skin and planting fear
He had seen too many of his brothers hang from trees
Swaying back and forth like the waves in the sea
   Back and forth until they reached their home
   And were finally free
And still he dreamed
   Always hearing her beat
But now he dreamed for freedom
And prayed for swift feet
   He gathered his wife and child
And as the sunset they escaped with the night
He followed the North Star until he was free
Never once looking back, never wanting to see
He was now a free man
His dream in his hand

Years passed a new day arrived

Slavery was gone but prejudice arises

    Whips replaced by water hoses

    And constant signs telling coloreds NO

But a new dream set in

One worth marching; one worth fighting

    For every man to be treated equal

    Despite his skin

A dream of many… that kept living

Years passed again

The signs were removed

    Now blacks and whites, yellows and reds

    Sat in the same school

The children of slaves are now

Doctors and lawyers, teachers and politicians

    We now sit at America's table

    Without being forced into the kitchen.

… And the dream lives on

A college student stands in a crowd …

In front of him stands a little boy holding his father's hand proud.

    And they eagerly wait—

Standing in a crowd among blacks, whites, Latinos, Asians

Muslims, Christians and Jews

As the world watched for a moment

All stood in the same shoes.

And then he appeared on the stage

A breath of good news ...

Barack Obama

Was now the forty-fourth president

Of the United States of America

He is delivering a dream NOW—

It now lives on in that college student,

In that little boy, and it now lives on in us.

From the beginning there's always been a dream ...

I thank God Martin Luther King, Jr., planted his seed.

Dreams are unwavering, hard to be broken,

Not easily cast into the shadows of solitude

No dreams keep growing until they come true.

Only you can release the dream inside of you

The dream lives on! The dream Lives on!

I can stand on every mountain top and shout
Yes the dream does live on!

To My African Warrior

I am Africa and you are my African warrior snatched from my
womb
Taken away from me before you were able to bloom
You have yet to see my beauty with your own eyes
But your soul knows that I am the one that flows great Niles

My lost African warrior
I know you hear my cries

You use to walk pride lands
Now you're the property of an American man
Trapped in a systematic jungle of so called "democracy"
A sophisticated name given to what we know as slavery

My poor African warrior I beg to you fight!
Don't be blinded into giving your life

I have seen plantation fields change into penitentiary yards
With my children still locked in chains behind prison bars
Run my child run

Stand up and stop being controlled by poison

To my African warrior
I need you back home
It is I Africa your mother, wife, sister, and your Queen
Strong African warrior return and be my King

I have never stopped looking for you after all of these years
Has time made you forget what you have left here?
My African warrior I still sing for you to come home
All of Africa will glow when her warrior takes his throne

And this is to my African warrior.

TRUTH

EMERGENCY CALL

-911 What's your emergency?

-911 What's your emergency?

The operator calmly asked

As I tried to sort the facts

There in front of me laid a black man dying

There in front of me a whole race was lying

Society had fired one shot into the heart

And now he lay breathless with his life cut short

There I was trying to revive him

Doing CPR calling 911, but life didn't seem to be inside of him

It didn't have to be this way

Since day one he knew society wanted it to be this way

Like a lion in the jungle he was hunted

He was strong so a bounty was set and he was wanted

Many times before they tried to kill him

Just look at his history and see where he's been

They kidnapped him in shackles and chains

Packed him like a package and shipped him to a new land

Where they stripped him of his heritage and gave him a new
name

Slave was his classification and nigger was his shame.

With whips they beat him and from ropes he hung
Society had it out for him since Day One
But he survived slavery to be attacked by poverty
Constantly being robbed by the million dollar lottery
But poverty compared nothing to slavery
So society sent out its Calvary
Crack…..
A friend of the moment but an enemy to the end
Now do you understand it when I say just look at where he's
been
When all else has failed society recruited his brother
Plotted blacks against blacks—
Letting them kill each other
Provided guns in hoods already flooded by crack
But not even that could hold the black man back
Because he fought to be free
Marched to be equal
Organized to prevail and vocalized for the people
But lately society has been running him down
Must have talked to his sister
Because he hasn't been coming around
Guess she told his secrets and exposed his weaknesses
So society devised a new plan
On how to kill the black man

It took him and glorified him

Gave him sports contracts and record deals

Put him on TV and told him how to feel

Made him act a certain way, dress a certain way and told him how

to think

It used him to advertise sin

Let him rap about being a rap star and a p-i-m-p

Gave him money and expensive jewelry

They made it cool to rap about sex but HIV never got a bar

But society's made it the main attraction the up and coming star

Now the black man's not who he use to be

The bad outnumber the good and the masses speak

And here he lies in front of me

I've always been his backbone

He and I have a history

   -911 What's your emergency?

He's dying He's dying and just as I start to cry

The black man I've known all of my life

Opens his eye to give it one more try

Live, Live, Live.

5 Stars

What are little girls made of?
Sugar and spice and everything that's nice.
That's what little girls are made of in "fairy tale" world.
But instead she lives in reality where her mother plays make
believe
And tries to be something other than mommy!
She's more concerned with nails and toes
Late night caps and scandalous clothes

She rather popping bottles than making bottles
Posting half naked pics on MySpace like she is a top model
Biting off to much at once makes life a tough swallow

But she's a Five Star chick
Just check out her fit
Hair and nails did; in the club doing it real big
Only problem is she's forgetting her kids!

What do little girls dream about?

Being just like mommy
So she sticks her back out trying to emulate sexy
Dancing in the mirror singing rap songs

Calling up her boyfriend on her Dora phone

If her mommy can do it, why can't she?

Baby girl's eyes have been blinded before she could see

Barbie dolls are remaining on Wal-Mart shelves

Because some young mothers are concerned with only themselves.

Constantly losing sight chasing after males

But she's a Five Star chick

Just check out her fit

Hair and nails did; in the club doing it real big

Only problem is she's forgetting her kids!

Now baby girl wants to club like her momma does

Because she believes that's the only way she'll get love

And so the cycle begins

Due to reckless women

What are little girls made of?

The things their mother show them!

Life

Everyday many people venture off into this thing called "life". They become so caught up in "life" that they forget to LIVE. They're simply going through movements. They inhale without breathing, blink without seeing, sleep without dreaming, and eat without feeding their soul. What is the purpose of life if you don't live it? Breathe deeply; live fully!

Black Diamonds

I call them black diamonds, like blood diamonds they're
forever shining.
Even in death they're eternal blinding
And I'm still trying
To figure out why we bring about all of this dying
Mother's crying
Praying to God asking why and
Why are we fighting?

Broken mother begging for one more heart beat, one last breath
Screaming Dear Lord raise him like Nazareth
Weeping mother wanting her son back
But a bullet to the back of the head, can't reverse that

My brother made the news
While his mother made her debut
She is now lady sing the blues
Her audience filling cold wooden pews
As the preacher delivers a premature eulogy
Fans waving back and forth cutting through misery
Like a hurricane meeting the gulf's thick air
Heavy is her despair

Black Diamonds

Gone before they realized they were shining

Dreams never lived

Often left to be fulfilled in fatherless kids

Black Diamond

You'll never stop shining

All of this pressure is going to make you more vibrant

My beautiful Black Diamonds

Mister

Mister, why did you beat her? Why did you black her eye and blue her heart?
Why did you make her cry and tear her apart?
Mister, why did you beat her?

Mister do you love your kids? Then why did you break in doors and punch in holes? You left them crying; did you not hear?
Or was your anger too much to notice tears?
Mister, do you love your kids?

Mister what were you trying to prove?
You're angry at the world
Tossing it away like dice not afraid to lose
Pain is not love; love is not pain
Life's far from a game
But you're steady playing
Mister, what were you trying to prove?

Mister, why did you drag her by her hair? Did you not hear her screams?

Why did you kick her to the ground? I thought she was your
queen
Why did you punch her like a man? Did you want to see her face
bleed?
Why did you have to grab your gun? Didn't you hear her make
pleads?

You vowed to love and protect her
Not beat and neglect her
You vowed until death do you apart
 Not a bullet through her heart.

Mister, is this really how love is suppose to feel?
I'm not asking for much; only for you to keep it real?

Mister, please think about it!

What's Your Name Boy?

There he goes rocking his white-T

Low top, high top air forces and a fold of dope money

He thinks he's real hard a true playa to the game

But the truth of the matter is he doesn't even know his name.

So, what's your name boy?

--Toby

That's what it is

Because you're no Counta Kinte' you're just faking it

It's a disgrace that you're painted in black

Because you're pushing us back

You're supposed to lead us to our homeland

Raise us all from oppression

But you're no real black man

It's a shoe you can't fill

Because you're too busy keeping it real

Society's got your mind messed up

Have you living the line of a rap song

Yeah you don't give a -----

Don't you know we've been set free?

Then why do you choose to remain a slave to society

Hey what's your name boy?

Toby, that's what it is.

Because Counta Kinte' wouldn't choose to live like this

What's your name boy?

Can't you hear the drums calling?

What's your name boy?

Don't you feel the blood pumping?

What's your name boy?

It's easy to be Toby, but harder to be free

What's your name boy?

Is it Toby or Counta Kinte' ….Which is it going to be?

What's your name boy?

LEARNING
LIFE

Woe betides the man who plants his seeds without watering them. They will still grow beautiful and strong. In their blooming he will wither because they will not know him.

If we live solely by what we are told than we will forever be blind.

*My heart bleeds from the turmoil
I see. What has happened to life?*

Giving in is easy; it's the fighting that is hard. There is never a victory without first a battle. When you are down to your last remember victory is within your reach.
Keep Fighting!

If I would have listened to them they would have defeated me. I refuse to be silent. "They" only have as much power as YOU give them.

The mind is a muscle that must be constantly exercised to stay strong because if left weak it will be overpowered by anything.

Sometimes you have to lose yourself to find your true self.

The mind of the human race will never be fully understood.
People are far too complex for understanding.

America's problem is that its people over indulge.

A person that lacks self discipline seals his death.

Even if a man lives in Utopia he will still find something else he longs for.

If the government is supposed to be for the people then why are so many unrepresented?

Deep down inside everyone has the key to succeed in life…. that key is God. Many doors remain locked because so many have lost that key.

A mind that cultivates great thoughts but doesn't harvest is wasteful.

Lips that speak false truths can be more deadly that a gun but, lips that praise the Lord can never be harmed.

If you're constantly carrying someone eventually they become excess baggage. Sometimes it's better to leave them at claims so that they may find themselves.

Never entertain foolish men, their ignorance is like venom.

You don't just wake up one morning to find that you've arrived at your destiny. No, you push your way there after a long journey with eyes wide open refusing to sleep.

Beware because snakes may shed their skin but they remain the same within.

If once upon a time was different I wonder if I would still be here wishing. But my once upon a time has been written; I thank God my book is far from finished.

If you want to know the truth then observe. Observation reveals all truth.

A dream is merely a dream if it is only seen behind closed eyes. It is with eyes wide open that we touch the untouchable in starry night skies. Everyone has wings but not everyone chooses to fly.

I wonder why some people choose to live blindly when God has blessed them with sight.

Do not chase your hunger for this world it will leave you empty. Instead chase your hunger for the Lord. Only he can fill you.

If you don't know yourself you will easily be conquered. The enemy is always watching therefore he knows you. There is strength in knowing who you really are.

It is easy for the weak to accept defeat because they lack strength but it's a pity when the strong go silently into the night.

The man that seeks to know the world but fails to know himself is hopeless and forever will remain searching.

Dreams come to those with sleepy eyes, but success seldomly know sleep once those dreams come to life.

The mind is like a room. It can either be lit with light or remain dormant in darkness.

It's easy to distinguish an untrained mouth. It inadvertently speaks prematurely and exposes the motives of the mind. Yes, loose lips are a curse.

My sheet waits like a blank canvas thirsting for colors and longing for life. As my pen connects my soul begins to write. I create a Masterpiece with my words I write, I write, I write!

I AM AFRICA

I AM AFRICA

I stand before you baring my soul
Yes, I am Africa my being is eternal
When I walk you can hear African drums calling
Beating boom, boom, boom
And when I stand still it's like the universe is falling

FOR I AM AFRICA

The dark midnight skies are trapped within my eyes
If you peer deep enough you will become mesmerized
And captured in my paradise

I AM AFRICA

My skin glows from the gold that I hold
And diamonds from within my mines are scattered in my soul
Within my boundaries the greatest river flows
And the fertile land grows
The freshest fruit you will ever taste
Nectar juice dripping down your face
There's no strange fruit in my land
No tree ornaments to be hung by any man

I AM AFRICA

I have birthed a nation
The strongest woman in creation
My sons have been Kings
My daughters have been Queens
I've had life snatched from my womb to be shipped overseas
To become slaves on a plantation of so called democracy

I AM AFRICA

Motionless I stand praying for them
Voiceless I cry from the slaying of them

BUT I AM AFRICA

I am Angela and Ann
Brenda and Claudia
Dinah and Emily
Faye and Gail
Hilda and Irene
Josephine and Kenya
Larhonda and Melissa
Natalie and Oprah
Phyliss and Queen
Rosa and Shelia
Teresa and Ursula
Velma and Whitney
Xenobia
Yvonne and Zora

I walk like Africa
I talk like Africa
I eat like Africa
I breathe like Africa
When I lay my head down at night I even sleep like Africa
I laugh like Africa
I pray like Africa
But most of all I love like Africa

I AM AFRICA

BEHIND CLOSED EYES

About the Author

Micaela Mone' is a poet from Eunice, Louisiana. Her style of writing is best described as soul writing because she speaks from life experiences. Her ultimate goal in life is to raise her two sons into positive, honest, and selfless men. She has been quoted saying "When my stay here is over I want to leave knowing that I gave hope to someone else. Then, I will know my destiny was fulfilled. She is currently working on her second poetry book. More info on this author can be found on her website Micaela-Mone.com.

Made in the USA
Charleston, SC
06 October 2010